ANGUILLA TRAVEL GUIDE

2024

Discover Anguilla: Your Companion To Caribbean Paradise And Unforgettable Experiences - Insider Tips For Island Bliss.

BY

Mia Aurora

Copyright

Table Of Contents

Copyrighted Page

CHAPTER ONE

Introduction To Anguilla

1.1. Welcome To Anguilla

Anguilla, a British Overseas Territory, is a Caribbean island known for its pristine beaches, turquoise waters, and laid-back atmosphere. It is located in the Eastern Caribbean, just north of Saint Kitts and Nevis. Anguilla is a small island, measuring only 16 miles long and three miles wide, but it is packed with things to see and do.

Beaches

Anguilla has over 33 beaches, all of which are public. Some of the most popular beaches include Shoal Bay Beach, Meads Bay Beach, and Rendezvous Bay Beach. These beaches are known for their soft white sand, clear turquoise waters, and gentle waves.

Activities

In addition to swimming and sunbathing, there are many other activities to enjoy in Anguilla. Visitors can go snorkeling, diving, fishing, sailing, and kayaking. There are also several golf courses and tennis courts on the island.

Food and Drink

Anguilla has a diverse culinary scene, with restaurants serving everything from fresh seafood to international cuisine. Some of the most popular dishes include lobster, conch, and johnnycakes. Visitors can also enjoy a variety of rum drinks and cocktails.

Culture

Anguilla has a rich culture that is influenced by its African, European, and Caribbean heritage. Visitors can learn more about Anguillian culture by visiting the Heritage Museum, attending a cultural event, or simply chatting with the friendly locals.

No matter what your interests are, you're sure to find something to love in Anguilla. So welcome to paradise!

NOTE

As of October 2023, Anguilla is open to tourists from all over the world. There are no COVID-19 testing or vaccination requirements for entry. However, visitors are required to complete a health declaration form and purchase travel insurance.

Anguilla is a safe and welcoming destination. The crime rate is low, and the locals are friendly and helpful. However, it is always important to be aware of your surroundings and take precautions to protect your belongings.

Anguilla is a beautiful and diverse island with something to offer everyone. Whether you're looking for a relaxing beach vacation, an active adventure, or a cultural experience, you're sure to find it in Anguilla.

1.2. History And Culture

Anguilla is a British Overseas Territory located in the Eastern Caribbean. It is known for its pristine beaches, turquoise waters, and laid-back atmosphere. However, Anguilla has a rich history and culture that is often overlooked by visitors.

History

The earliest inhabitants of Anguilla were the Arawak people, who arrived on the island around 2000 BC. The Arawak were a peaceful people who lived in harmony with nature. They were skilled farmers and fishermen, and they also created beautiful pottery and other artifacts.

In 1493, Christopher Columbus became the first European to sight Anguilla. However, the island was not colonized until 1650, when British settlers from Saint Kitts arrived. The British brought enslaved Africans to Anguilla to work on the island's plantations.

Anguilla remained under British rule for centuries. However, in the 1960s, the Anguillan people began to demand independence. In 1967, Anguilla seceded from Saint Kitts and Nevis, but the British government refused to recognize Anguilla's independence.

In 1969, the Anguillan people staged a revolution. They expelled the British police force and declared themselves an independent republic. However, the British government responded by sending troops to Anguilla. The British troops remained in Anguilla for four years, until 1973.

In 1976, Anguilla became a British Overseas Territory. This gave Anguilla some autonomy, but the British government still retained control over certain matters, such as defense and foreign affairs.

Culture

Anguilla's culture is a unique blend of African, European, and Caribbean influences. The island's official language is English, but many Anguillians also speak a dialect of English known as Anguillian Creole.

Anguillan cuisine is also a blend of different cultures. Popular dishes include lobster, conch, and johnnycakes. Anguilla is also known for its rum drinks and cocktails.

Anguillians are friendly and welcoming people. They are proud of their culture and heritage, and they are always happy to share it with visitors.

1.3. Geography And Climate

Anguilla is a British Overseas Territory located in the Eastern Caribbean. It is a small island, measuring only 16 miles long and three miles wide. Anguilla is known for its pristine beaches, turquoise waters, and laid-back atmosphere.

Geography

Anguilla is a flat island with a maximum elevation of only 210 feet. The island is composed of coral and limestone, and its soil is thin and poor. This makes it difficult to grow crops in Anguilla, and the island is largely dependent on imported food.

Anguilla is surrounded by a number of uninhabited islets and cays. The largest of these is Sombrero Island, which is located about 30 miles north of Anguilla.

Climate

Anguilla has a tropical wet and dry climate. The average temperature is 27 degrees Celsius (80 degrees Fahrenheit) year-round. The rainy season runs from July to October, with the wettest months being September and October. The dry season runs from November to June, with the driest months being February and March.

Anguilla is vulnerable to hurricanes, which can occur from June to November. The peak hurricane season is from August to mid-October.

Environmental issues

Anguilla faces a number of environmental challenges, including:

Coastal erosion: Anguilla's beaches are vulnerable to erosion caused by sea level rise and storms.

Water pollution: Anguilla's water resources are vulnerable to pollution from sewage and agricultural runoff.

Loss of biodiversity: Anguilla's natural habitats are under threat from development and climate change.

Conservation efforts

The Anguilla government and a number of non-governmental organizations are working to address Anguilla's environmental challenges. Some of the conservation efforts underway include:

Beach restoration projects: These projects are designed to protect Anguilla's beaches from erosion.

Water treatment plants: These plants are being built to improve the quality of Anguilla's water resources.

Protected areas: The Anguilla government has established a number of protected areas to conserve the island's biodiversity.

Anguilla is a beautiful and fragile island. The Anguillan people are committed to protecting their island for future generations.

CHAPTER TWO

Planning Your Trip

2.1. When To Visit

Anguilla is a British Overseas Territory in the Caribbean. It is a popular tourist destination known for its white-sand beaches, crystal-clear waters, and laid-back atmosphere. The best time to visit Anguilla is during the dry season, which runs from December to April. During these months, the weather is sunny and warm, with average temperatures in the mid-80s Fahrenheit. There is also less rainfall during the dry season, making it ideal for beach activities and other outdoor pursuits.

Benefits of visiting Anguilla during the dry season

Ideal weather: The dry season is the best time to enjoy Anguilla's beautiful weather. With average temperatures in the mid-80s Fahrenheit and sunny skies, you can spend your days relaxing on the beach, swimming in the ocean, and exploring the island.

Less rainfall: The dry season is also the time of year with the least rainfall. This means that you can enjoy your vacation without having to worry about rain showers ruining your plans.

More activities and events: The dry season is also the peak tourist season in Anguilla, so there are more activities and events to choose from. This includes everything from boat tours and snorkeling excursions to live music performances and cultural festivals.

Other factors to consider when planning your trip to Anguilla

Hurricane season: The hurricane season in Anguilla runs from June to November. While it is possible to have a wonderful vacation during the hurricane season, it is important to be aware of the risks and to take precautions. For example, you should purchase travel insurance and monitor the weather forecast closely.

Holiday season: The holiday season (December to January) is the busiest time of year in Anguilla. If you are planning to visit during this time, it is important to book your flights and accommodations well in advance.

Budget: Anguilla is a relatively expensive destination, especially during the peak season. However, there are ways to save money, such as staying in a villa or apartment, cooking your own meals, and taking advantage of free activities.

Tips for planning your trip to Anguilla

Book your flights and accommodations in advance, especially if you are traveling during the peak season.

Purchase travel insurance to protect yourself against unexpected events, such as hurricanes.

Monitor the weather forecast closely, especially if you are traveling during the hurricane season.

Pack for all types of weather, even if you are traveling during the dry season.

Bring sunscreen, insect repellent, and a hat to protect yourself from the sun.

Be prepared for high prices, especially during the peak season.

Consider renting a car to explore the island at your own pace.

Take advantage of free activities, such as hiking, swimming, and sunbathing.

2.2. Visa And Entry Requirements

Anguilla is a British Overseas Territory in the Caribbean. Citizens of most countries can visit Anguilla for up to 90 days without a visa. However, there are a few exceptions, so it is important to check the requirements for your country of citizenship before you travel.

Visa requirements

Citizens of the following countries do not need a visa to visit Anguilla:

Antigua and Barbuda, Bahamas, Barbados, Belize, Bermuda, British Overseas Territories (other than Anguilla), Canada, Cayman Islands, Dominica, Falkland Islands, Grenada,Guyana,Jamaica, Montserrat, New Zealand, St. Kitts and Nevis,
St. Lucia, St. Vincent and the Grenadines, Turks and Caicos Islands, United Kingdom, and United States.

Citizens of all other countries must apply for a visa to visit Anguilla. Visa applications can be made online or at a British Embassy or High Commission.

Entry requirements

In addition to a valid passport, all visitors to Anguilla must also have:

- A return or onward ticket

- Confirmation of accommodation

- Evidence of sufficient funds to support your stay

- You may also be asked to show proof of vaccination against certain diseases, such as yellow fever.

Other important information

- Visitors to Anguilla must be at least 18 years old.

- Minors must be traveling with a parent or guardian.

- Visitors must declare all goods and currency that they are bringing into Anguilla.

- A departure tax is payable when leaving Anguilla.

- Tips for entering Anguilla

Arrive at Anguilla Clayton J. Lloyd International Airport
(AXA) at least two hours before your flight is scheduled
to depart.

Have all of your travel documents ready, including your
passport, return or onward ticket, confirmation of
accommodation, and evidence of sufficient funds.

Be prepared to answer questions about your trip, such as
how long you plan to stay in Anguilla and what you plan
to do while you are there.

Be polite and respectful to immigration officials.

2.3. Travel Insurance

Travel insurance is a type of insurance that protects you
against unexpected events while you are traveling. It can
cover a wide range of things, such as medical expenses,
trip cancellation, lost luggage, and rental car damage.

Whether or not you need travel insurance for Anguilla
depends on a number of factors, including your
nationality, your health, your travel plans, and your
budget. However, there are a few general things to keep
in mind:

Anguilla is a relatively expensive destination. Medical expenses can be especially high, so travel insurance can be a good way to protect yourself against financial hardship in the event of an accident or illness.

Anguilla is located in the Caribbean, which is a hurricane-prone region. Travel insurance can help to cover the costs of trip cancellation or interruption if your trip is affected by a hurricane.

Anguilla is a popular tourist destination, but it is still relatively small and isolated. This means that medical facilities may not be as extensive or sophisticated as in other countries. Travel insurance can provide you with access to quality medical care, even if you are in a remote area.

Here are some specific benefits of travel insurance for Anguilla tourists:

Medical coverage: Medical coverage is one of the most important benefits of travel insurance. It can cover the costs of hospitalization, doctor visits, prescription medications, and other medical expenses.

Trip cancellation and interruption coverage: Trip cancellation and interruption coverage can reimburse you for the cost of your trip if you are unable to travel or must return home early due to an unforeseen event, such as a medical emergency, family emergency, or flight cancellation.

Lost luggage coverage: Lost luggage coverage can reimburse you for the value of your lost luggage, up to a certain limit.

Rental car damage coverage: Rental car damage coverage can reimburse you for the cost of repairing or replacing a rental car that is damaged or stolen while you are traveling.

How to choose a travel insurance policy

When choosing a travel insurance policy, it is important to compare different plans and find one that meets your specific needs. You should also consider the following factors:

The type of coverage you need: Decide which types of coverage are most important to you, such as medical coverage, trip cancellation and interruption coverage, lost luggage coverage, and rental car damage coverage.

The cost of the policy: Travel insurance policies can vary in price depending on the type of coverage you choose and the length of your trip. It is important to compare different plans to find one that fits your budget.

The reputation of the insurance company: Choose an insurance company with a good reputation. You can read reviews online or ask for recommendations from friends and family.

2.4. Currency And Banking

The official currency of Anguilla is the Eastern Caribbean dollar (EC$). It is pegged to the US dollar at a fixed exchange rate of EC$2.70 to US$1. US dollars are widely accepted in Anguilla, and many businesses will give you change in both EC$ and US$.

Banking in Anguilla

Anguilla has a modern banking system with a number of commercial banks and offshore banks. The following banks have branches in Anguilla:

Bank of Anguilla

- FirstCaribbean International Bank (Barbados) Limited

- National Commercial Bank of Anguilla Limited

- Scotiabank Anguilla Limited

These banks offer a range of banking services, including personal and business accounts, loans, and investment products.

ATMs

ATMs are widely available in Anguilla, and you can use your international debit or credit card to withdraw EC$ from most ATMs.

Currency exchange

You can exchange currency at banks, hotels, and some currency exchange bureaus. Banks typically offer the best exchange rates, but they may charge a commission. Currency exchange bureaus may offer slightly lower exchange rates, but they usually do not charge a commission.

Tips for managing your money in Anguilla

- Budget for your trip and track your spending.

- Bring a mix of EC$ and US dollars.

- Use your international debit or credit card to withdraw cash from ATMs.

- Be aware of the exchange rate and compare rates before exchanging currency.

- Keep your money and valuables safe.

2.5. Language And Communication

The official language of Anguilla is English. However, the majority of the population speaks a dialect of English known as Anguillian Creole. Anguillian Creole is a unique language that has been influenced by English, African languages, and Spanish.

Anguillian Creole is spoken in a variety of contexts, including at home, at work, and in social settings. It is also used in some government and educational settings. Standard English is used in formal settings, such as in schools, businesses, and government offices. It is also used in the media and in religious services.

Communication in Anguilla

Anguillians are generally friendly and welcoming people. They are also known for being laid-back and easygoing.

If you are visiting Anguilla, it is helpful to learn a few basic Anguillian Creole phrases. This will show that you are making an effort to connect with the local culture.

However, it is important to note that Anguillians are generally happy to speak English with visitors. So, even if you don't know any Anguillian Creole, you will still be able to communicate with people.

Here are a few tips for communicating in Anguilla:

- Be polite and respectful.

- Speak slowly and clearly.

- If you are unsure of how to say something, ask.

- Be patient and understanding.

CHAPTER THREE

Getting To Anguilla

3.1. Airports And Airlines

Anguilla is a British Overseas Territory located in the Eastern Caribbean Sea. It is a popular tourist destination known for its beautiful beaches, crystal-clear waters, and luxurious resorts.

There are two ways to get to Anguilla by air:

- Direct flights to Anguilla (AXA)

Direct flights to Anguilla are available from the following airports:

Miami International Airport (MIA)

John F. Kennedy International Airport (JFK)

Atlanta Hartsfield-Jackson International Airport (ATL)

American Airlines and Delta Air Lines offer direct flights to Anguilla from these airports. The flight time is approximately 3 hours and 30 minutes from Miami and 4 hours and 30 minutes from New York and Atlanta.

- Fly to St. Maarten (SXM) and take a ferry to Anguilla

St. Maarten is a neighboring island to Anguilla located just 10 miles away. There are many airlines that offer direct flights to St. Maarten from major cities in the United States, Canada, and Europe.

Once you arrive in St. Maarten, you can take a ferry to Anguilla. The ferry ride takes approximately 20 minutes. There are several ferry companies that operate between St. Maarten and Anguilla, including Seaborne Airlines, Tradewind Aviation, and Air Sunshine.

Which option is best for you?

The best option for you will depend on your budget and preferences. If you are looking for the most convenient and fastest way to get to Anguilla, then flying direct is the best option. However, direct flights can be more expensive.

If you are on a budget or want to have more flexibility with your travel dates, then flying to St. Maarten and taking a ferry is a good option. Ferry tickets are typically less expensive than airline tickets, and there are more ferry departures to choose from.

Tips for getting to Anguilla

Book your flights and ferry tickets in advance, especially if you are traveling during peak season.

Arrive at the airport or ferry terminal at least two hours before your scheduled departure time.

Be sure to have your passport and other travel documents in order.

If you are flying to St. Maarten and taking a ferry to Anguilla, be sure to factor in the time it will take to clear customs and immigration on both islands.

Whichever option you choose, be sure to book your flights and ferry tickets in advance and arrive at the airport or ferry terminal early. With its beautiful beaches, crystal-clear waters, and luxurious resorts, Anguilla is a great destination for a relaxing and unforgettable vacation.

3.2. Ferry Services

Anguilla is a beautiful island in the Caribbean Sea, known for its white-sand beaches, crystal-clear waters, and luxurious resorts. There are two main ways to get to Anguilla: by plane or by ferry.

Ferry services to Anguilla

There are two ferry ports in Anguilla: Blowing Point Ferry Terminal on the south side of the island and Sandy Ground Ferry Terminal on the north side of the island.

Ferries from St. Maarten

The most popular way to get to Anguilla by ferry is from the neighboring island of St. Maarten. There are several ferry companies that operate between St. Maarten and Anguilla, including Seaborne Airlines, Tradewind Aviation, and Air Sunshine. The ferry ride takes approximately 20 minutes.

Ferries from other islands

There are also ferry services to Anguilla from other Caribbean islands, such as St. Kitts, Nevis, and St. Thomas. However, these ferry services are less frequent and may require longer travel times.

Booking your ferry ticket

You can book your ferry ticket online or at the ferry terminal. It is recommended to book your ticket in advance, especially if you are traveling during peak season.

What to expect on the ferry

The ferries to Anguilla are typically modern and comfortable. They offer amenities such as restrooms, snacks, and drinks. Some ferries also offer free Wi-Fi.

Arrival in Anguilla

Once you arrive in Anguilla, you will need to clear customs and immigration. This process is typically quick and easy.

Tips for getting to Anguilla by ferry

Book your ferry ticket in advance, especially if you are traveling during peak season.

Arrive at the ferry terminal at least 30 minutes before your scheduled departure time.

Be sure to have your passport and other travel documents in order.

If you are bringing luggage, be sure to tag it clearly with your name and contact information.

Enjoy the scenic ferry ride to Anguilla!

3.3. Getting Around The Island

Anguilla is a small island in the Caribbean Sea, with a population of just over 15,000 people. It is known for its beautiful beaches, crystal-clear waters, and luxurious resorts.

There are a few different ways to get around Anguilla, each with its own price range.

Taxis

Taxis are the most convenient way to get around Anguilla, but they can also be the most expensive. Taxis are not metered, and fares are set by the government.

Here are some of the average taxi fares in Anguilla:

From the airport to West End: $20-$25

From West End to Sandy Ground: $15-$20

From Sandy Ground to Shoal Bay: $25-$30

From Shoal Bay to Blowing Point: $20-$25

Rental cars

Renting a car is a good option if you want to explore the island at your own pace. There are several car rental companies in Anguilla, and the rates are generally competitive.

Here are some of the average car rental rates in Anguilla:

Economy car: $50-$75 per day

Midsize car: $75-$100 per day

SUV: $100-$125 per day

Public transportation

Anguilla has a limited public transportation system, consisting of buses and vans. The buses and vans run on fixed routes and schedules, and the fares are very reasonable.

Here are some of the average public transportation fares in Anguilla:

Bus ride: $2-$3

Van ride: $3-$4

Other options

Other options for getting around Anguilla include:

Bicycles: Bicycles can be rented for around $10 per day.
Scooters: Scooters can be rented for around $20 per day.

Water taxis: Water taxis can be hired to take you to different parts of the island. The fares vary depending on the distance traveled.

Tips for getting around Anguilla

If you are staying at a resort, ask the concierge about the best way to get around the island. Many resorts offer shuttle services to popular destinations.
If you are renting a car, be sure to drive on the left side of the road.

If you are using public transportation, be sure to check the schedules in advance.

Be sure to wear sunscreen and a hat when getting around the island, as the sun can be very strong.

CHAPTER FOUR

Accommodation

4.1. Resorts And Hotels

Anguilla is a British Overseas Territory in the Eastern Caribbean Sea. It is known for its pristine beaches, turquoise waters, and laid-back atmosphere. Anguilla is also a very safe destination, with a low crime rate.

Here are some of the best and safest resorts and hotels in Anguilla, along with their location and price range:

Luxury Resorts

Four Seasons Resort and Residences Anguilla: Located on Barnes Bay, this resort offers luxurious accommodations, stunning views, and world-class amenities. Price range: $1,250-$5,000 per night.

Belmond Cap Juluca: This iconic resort is located on Maundays Bay and is known for its white-sand beach and Moorish-style architecture. Price range: $870-$2,500 per night.

Zemi Beach House, LXR Hotels & Resorts: This boutique resort is located on Shoal Bay Beach and offers spacious suites, a world-class spa, and a variety of dining options. Price range: $890-$2,000 per night.

Mid-Range Resorts

Aurora Anguilla Resort & Golf Club: This resort is located on Long Bay Beach and offers a variety of accommodations, including villas, suites, and hotel rooms. It also has a golf course, tennis courts, and a variety of other amenities. Price range: $500-$1,500 per night.

Tranquility Beach Anguilla: This boutique resort is located on Meads Bay Beach and offers spacious suites, a private beach, and a variety of dining options. Price range: $625-$1,500 per night.

Anguilla Great House Beach Resort: This resort is located on Rendezvous Bay and offers a variety of accommodations, including villas, suites, and hotel rooms. It also has a private beach, a spa, and a variety of other amenities. Price range: $400-$1,000 per night.

Budget-Friendly Hotels

Turtle's Nest Beach Resort: This hotel is located on Shoal Bay Beach and offers a variety of accommodations, including studios, suites, and villas. It also has a private beach, a pool, and a restaurant. Price range: $250-$750 per night.

Shoal Bay Villas: This hotel is located on Shoal Bay Beach and offers a variety of villas and apartments. It also has a private beach, a pool, and a restaurant. Price range: $200-$500 per night.

Anguilla Palms Hotel: This hotel is located in the town of The Valley and offers a variety of rooms and suites. It also has a pool, a restaurant, and a bar. Price range: $150-$300 per night.

All of the resorts and hotels listed above are highly rated by guests and have a good reputation for safety and security. They are also all located in convenient areas, close to beaches, restaurants, and other attractions.

When choosing a resort or hotel in Anguilla, it is important to consider your budget and your travel preferences. If you are looking for a luxurious experience, one of the high-end resorts is a good option. If you are on a tighter budget, there are also a number of mid-range and budget-friendly hotels to choose from.

No matter what your budget is, you are sure to find a safe and comfortable place to stay in Anguilla.

4.2. Villas And Vacation Rentals

Anguilla is a British Overseas Territory in the Eastern Caribbean Sea. It is known for its pristine beaches, turquoise waters, and laid-back atmosphere. Anguilla is also a popular destination for luxury villas and vacation rentals.

Here are some of the best villas and vacation rentals in Anguilla, along with their location and price range:

Luxury Villas

Villa Alegria: This luxury villa is located on Meads Bay Beach and offers stunning views of the ocean. It has six bedrooms, seven bathrooms, a private pool, and a variety of other amenities. Price range: $1,500-$5,000 per night.

Villa Amarilla: This luxury villa is located on Sandy Hill and offers panoramic views of the island. It has five bedrooms, six bathrooms, a private pool, and a variety of other amenities. Price range: $1,200-$4,000 per night.

Villa Seaclusion: This luxury villa is located on Rendezvous Bay and offers direct access to the beach. It has four bedrooms, five bathrooms, a private pool, and a variety of other amenities. Price range: $1,000-$3,500 per night.

Mid-Range Villas

Villa Tranquility: This mid-range villa is located on Shoal Bay Beach and offers stunning views of the ocean. It has three bedrooms, three bathrooms, a private pool, and a variety of other amenities. Price range: $600-$2,000 per night.

Villa Serenity: This mid-range villa is located on Meads Bay Beach and offers direct access to the beach. It has four bedrooms, four bathrooms, a private pool, and a variety of other amenities. Price range: $500-$1,800 per night.

Villa Bella Vista: This mid-range villa is located on Rendezvous Bay and offers panoramic views of the island. It has three bedrooms, three bathrooms, a private pool, and a variety of other amenities. Price range: $400-$1,500 per night.

Budget-Friendly Vacation Rentals

Sandy Ground Villa: This budget-friendly vacation rental is located in the town of Sandy Ground and is close to beaches, restaurants, and shops. It has two bedrooms, two bathrooms, and a fully equipped kitchen. Price range: $200-$500 per night.

Shoal Bay East Villa: This budget-friendly vacation rental is located on Shoal Bay East Beach and offers direct access to the beach. It has one bedroom, one bathroom, and a fully equipped kitchen. Price range: $150-$400 per night.

West End Villa: This budget-friendly vacation rental is located on the west end of the island and offers stunning views of the ocean. It has two bedrooms, two bathrooms, and a fully equipped kitchen. Price range: $100-$300 per night.

No matter what your budget is, you are sure to find a villa or vacation rental in Anguilla that is perfect for you. Anguilla has a wide variety of villas and vacation rentals to choose from, so you are sure to find one that meets your needs and preferences.

When choosing a villa or vacation rental in Anguilla, it is important to consider your budget, your travel preferences, and the size of your group. If you are traveling with a large group, you may want to consider renting a villa. If you are on a tighter budget, a vacation rental may be a better option.

No matter what type of accommodation you choose, you are sure to have a wonderful time in Anguilla. Anguilla is a beautiful island with something to offer everyone.

4.3 Camping

Camping is not a popular activity in Anguilla, as there are no designated campgrounds on the island. However, there are a few places where you may be able to camp with permission from the landowner.

One option is to camp on the beach. However, it is important to note that most beaches in Anguilla are privately owned, so you will need to get permission from the landowner before camping. Additionally, it is important to be respectful of the environment and leave no trace behind.

Another option is to camp on private property. If you know someone who owns land in Anguilla, you may be able to get permission to camp on their property. However, it is important to be respectful of their property and leave no trace behind.

If you are planning on camping in Anguilla, it is important to be prepared for the elements. The weather in Anguilla can be hot and humid, so it is important to stay hydrated and wear sunscreen. Additionally, there can be mosquitoes in Anguilla, so it is important to use insect repellent.

Here are a few tips for camping in Anguilla:

Get permission from the landowner before camping. This is especially important if you are planning on camping on private property or on the beach.

Be respectful of the environment and leave no trace behind. This means packing out all of your trash and not harming the plants or animals.

Be prepared for the elements. The weather in Anguilla can be hot and humid, so it is important to stay hydrated and wear sunscreen. Additionally, there can be mosquitoes in Anguilla, so it is important to use insect repellent.

Bring all of your own supplies. There are no campgrounds in Anguilla, so you will need to bring your own tent, sleeping bag, and other camping supplies.

Here are a few places where you may be able to camp in Anguilla:

Little Bay Beach: This beach is located on the northeast coast of Anguilla and is known for its white sand and turquoise waters. It is also a popular spot for swimming, sunbathing, and snorkeling.

Sandy Hill Bay: This beach is located on the southwest coast of Anguilla and is known for its secluded atmosphere and stunning views of the Caribbean Sea. It is a great place to relax and escape the crowds.

Please note that these are just suggestions and there is no guarantee that you will be able to camp at any of these locations. It is always best to get permission from the landowner before camping.

Overall, camping in Anguilla is not a common activity and there are no designated campgrounds on the island. However, there are a few places where you may be able to camp with permission from the landowner. If you are planning on camping in Anguilla, it is important to be prepared for the elements and bring all of your own supplies.

CHAPTER FIVE

Things To Do

5.1. Beaches

Anguilla is a British overseas territory in the Caribbean Sea, known for its stunning beaches, crystal-clear waters, and laid-back atmosphere. The island has over 30 beaches to choose from, each with its own unique charm.

Here are the top Anguilla beaches, with price ranges and locations:

Shoal Bay Beach

Location: Northwest Anguilla

Price range: Free to access, with beach chairs and umbrellas available for rent

Shoal Bay Beach is consistently ranked as one of the best beaches in the world, and for good reason. It's a long stretch of white sand with turquoise waters that are perfect for swimming, sunbathing, and snorkeling. There are also several restaurants and bars located on the beach, so you can easily spend a whole day there.

Meads Bay

Location: Northwest Anguilla

Price range: Free to access, with beach chairs and umbrellas available for rent

Meads Bay is another popular beach in Anguilla, known for its wide expanse of sand and calm waters. It's a great place to relax and unwind, or to enjoy a romantic dinner at one of the many beachfront restaurants.

Little Bay

Location: Southwest Anguilla

Price range: Free to access, with beach chairs and umbrellas available for rent

Little Bay is a secluded beach that can only be accessed by boat or by climbing down a rope. It's a great place to escape the crowds and enjoy the peace and quiet. The water is also very clear, making it a great spot for swimming and snorkeling.

Rendezvous Bay

Location: Northeast Anguilla
Price range: Free to access, with beach chairs and umbrellas available for rent

Rendezvous Bay is a long, crescent-shaped beach with soft white sand and calm waters. It's a great place to swim, sunbathe, and go for walks along the beach. There are also several restaurants and bars located on the beach, so you can easily spend a whole day there.

Maundays Bay

Location: Southwest Anguilla

Price range: Free to access, with beach chairs and umbrellas available for rent

Maundays Bay is a small, secluded beach with white sand and clear blue waters. It's a great place to relax and escape the crowds. The beach is also home to several limestone caves, which are fun to explore.

Price ranges

The price range for Anguilla beaches can vary depending on the time of year and the specific beach. However, in general, the beaches in Anguilla are free to access. There may be a small fee for beach chairs and umbrellas, but this is typically very reasonable.

Tips for visiting Anguilla beaches

The best time to visit Anguilla is during the winter months, when the weather is warm and sunny.

Be sure to pack sunscreen, sunglasses, and a hat to protect yourself from the sun.

Bring water and snacks, as there may not be any vendors on all of the beaches.

Be respectful of the environment and leave no trace of your visit.

5.2. Water Activities

Anguilla is a British overseas territory in the Caribbean Sea, known for its stunning beaches, crystal-clear waters, and laid-back atmosphere. The island is also a great place to enjoy a variety of water activities, from swimming and sunbathing to snorkeling, diving, and sailing.

Here are the top Anguilla water activities, with price ranges and locations:

Snorkeling
Location: All over the island

Price range: $25-$50 per person

Anguilla is a great place to snorkel, with over 60 reefs to explore. Some of the best snorkeling spots include Shoal Bay, Rendezvous Bay, and Maundays Bay. You can book a snorkeling tour with a local operator, or rent your own snorkel gear and explore the reefs on your own.

Diving

Location: All over the island

Price range: $75-$150 per person

Anguilla is also a great place to dive, with over 30 dive sites to choose from. Some of the most popular dive sites include Sandy Island, Sombrero Island, and Dog Island. You can book a dive tour with a local operator, or get certified and dive on your own.

Sailing

Location: All over the island

Price range: $100-$300 per person

Anguilla is a great place to sail, with its calm waters and steady breezes. You can book a sailing charter with a local operator, or rent your own sailboat and explore the island at your own pace.

Fishing

Location: All over the island

Price range: $200-$500 per boat

Anguilla is a great place to fish, with a variety of fish species to catch, including tuna, marlin, and mahi-mahi. You can book a fishing charter with a local operator, or go fishing on your own from the shore or from a boat.

Other water activities

- Kayaking

- Stand-up paddleboarding

- Parasailing

- Jet skiing

- Windsurfing

- Kiteboarding

These activities are all available in Anguilla, and can be booked through local operators. Price ranges vary depending on the activity and the length of time you book.

Tips for enjoying water activities in Anguilla

Be sure to wear sunscreen, sunglasses, and a hat to protect yourself from the sun.

Drink plenty of water to stay hydrated.

Be aware of your surroundings and be careful of currents and rip tides.

Book your activities with reputable operators.

5.3. Land Activities

Anguilla is a British overseas territory in the Caribbean Sea, known for its stunning beaches, crystal-clear waters, and laid-back atmosphere. The island also has a variety of land activities to offer visitors, from hiking and biking to shopping and dining.

Here are the top Anguilla land activities, with price ranges and locations:

Hiking

Location: All over the island

Price range: Free

Anguilla has a variety of hiking trails to choose from, ranging from easy to challenging. Some of the most popular hiking trails include the Wallblake House Trail, the Crocus Bay Trail, and the Rendezvous Bay Trail.

Biking

Location: All over the island

Price range: $25-$50 per person per day
Anguilla is a great place to bike, with its flat terrain and smooth roads. You can rent a bike from a local operator and explore the island at your own pace.

Shopping

Location: The Valley, Sandy Ground, and West End

Price range: Varies
Anguilla has a variety of shops to choose from, selling everything from souvenirs to high-end fashion. Some of the best places to shop include The Valley Shopping Village, Sandy Ground Village, and West End Village.

Dining

Location: All over the island

Price range: Varies

Anguilla has a variety of restaurants to choose from, serving everything from Caribbean cuisine to international fare. Some of the most popular restaurants include Blanchard's, Straw Hat, and Veya.

Other land activities

- Visiting the Anguilla National Trust

- Exploring the Heritage Museum of Anguilla

- Playing golf at Anguilla Golf Course

- Visiting the Old Valley Church

- Taking a cooking class

- Going to a reggae party

These activities are all available in Anguilla, and can be booked through local operators or done independently. Price ranges vary depending on the activity.

Tips for enjoying land activities in Anguilla

Be sure to wear sunscreen, sunglasses, and a hat to protect yourself from the sun.

Drink plenty of water to stay hydrated.

Be respectful of the environment and leave no trace of your visit.

Book your activities with reputable operators.

5.4. Exploring Nature And Wildlife

Anguilla is a British overseas territory in the Caribbean Sea, known for its stunning beaches, crystal-clear waters, and laid-back atmosphere. The island is also home to a variety of unique natural and wildlife experiences.

Here are some of the best places to explore nature and wildlife in Anguilla:
Sombrero Island

Location: Off the northeast coast of Anguilla

Sombrero Island is a small uninhabited island located about 10 miles off the coast of Anguilla. It is a popular destination for snorkeling, diving, and birdwatching. The island is home to a variety of seabirds, including frigatebirds, boobies, and terns. It is also a breeding ground for sea turtles.

Sandy Island

Location: Off the southwest coast of Anguilla

Sandy Island is another small uninhabited island located off the coast of Anguilla. It is a popular destination for day trips and boat charters. The island is home to a beautiful white sand beach and crystal-clear waters. It is also a great spot for swimming, snorkeling, and sunbathing.

Anguilla National Trust

Location: The Valley, Anguilla

The Anguilla National Trust is a non-profit organization dedicated to protecting Anguilla's natural environment. The trust operates a number of nature reserves and sanctuaries, including the East End Marine Park, the

Sandy Island Marine Park, and the Shoal Bay Pond Reserve. The trust also offers a variety of nature tours and educational programs.

Wallblake House

Location: The Valley, Anguilla

Wallblake House is a historic plantation house that is now a museum. The house is surrounded by a beautiful garden that is home to a variety of plants and flowers. The garden is also a great place to see birds and other wildlife.

Other places to explore nature and wildlife in Anguilla:

- Crocus Hill

- Long Pond

- Rendezvous Bay

- Maundays Bay

- Meads Bay

Tips for exploring nature and wildlife in Anguilla:

Be respectful of the environment and leave no trace of your visit.

Wear sunscreen, sunglasses, and a hat to protect yourself from the sun.

Be aware of your surroundings and be careful of currents and rip tides.

Book your tours with reputable operators.

5.5. Nightlife And Entertainment

Anguilla may be known for its laid-back atmosphere, but that doesn't mean there's nothing to do at night. The island has a variety of nightlife and entertainment options to choose from, whether you're looking to dance the night away, enjoy a live music performance, or simply relax with a drink in hand.

Here are some of the best places to experience Anguilla's nightlife and entertainment:

Elvis Beach Bar

Location: Sandy Ground

Elvis Beach Bar is a popular spot for locals and tourists alike. The bar is located right on the beach and offers stunning views of the sunset. On weekends, there is live music and dancing.

The Dune Preserve

Location: Rendezvous Bay

The Dune Preserve is a unique bar and restaurant located on the beach. The bar is known for its live music and its eclectic atmosphere. The restaurant serves a variety of dishes, including Caribbean cuisine and seafood.

Lit Lounge

Location: Sandy Ground

Lit Lounge is a trendy bar and nightclub located in Sandy Ground. The club has a dance floor, a DJ, and a variety of drinks to choose from. There are also occasional events, such as fashion shows and themed nights.

Scilly Cay

Location: Sandy Island

Scilly Cay is a small island located off the coast of Anguilla. The island has a restaurant, a bar, and a beach. On Sundays, there is a live band and a barbecue.

Other places to experience Anguilla's nightlife and entertainment:

Pumphouse (Sandy Ground)

Straw Hat (Sandy Ground)

Bankie Banx's Dune Preserve (Rendezvous Bay)

Four Seasons Resort Anguilla (Meads Bay)

Belmond Cap Juluca (Maundays Bay)

Tips for enjoying Anguilla's nightlife and entertainment:

Be sure to dress appropriately for the venue you're visiting.

Drink plenty of water to stay hydrated.

Be aware of your surroundings and be careful of currents and riptides if you're swimming.

CHAPTER SIX

Dining And Cuisine

6.1. Local Anguillan Dishes

Anguilla is a small island in the Caribbean with a rich culinary culture. The local cuisine is influenced by African, European, and Native American traditions, resulting in a unique and flavorful mix of dishes.

Here are some of the most popular local Anguillan dishes, along with their price range:

Pigeon Peas and Rice

Pigeon peas and rice is the national dish of Anguilla. It is a hearty and flavorful dish made with pigeon peas, rice, and a variety of spices. Pigeon peas and rice is typically served with fried chicken, fish, or goat.

Price range: $10-$15 Location: Most restaurants in Anguilla serve pigeon peas and rice, but some of the best places to try it include:

Tasty's Restaurant (Sandy Ground)

Roy's Bayside Grill (West End)

The Barrel Stay (Sandy Ground)

Johnny Cakes

Johnny cakes are a type of flatbread that is popular in many Caribbean islands. They are made with flour, water, baking powder, and salt. Johnny cakes are typically eaten for breakfast, but they can also be served as a side dish with lunch or dinner.

Price range: $2-$3 Location: Johnny cakes can be found at most restaurants in Anguilla, but they are also widely available at grocery stores and bakeries.

Fried Fish

Anguilla is surrounded by water, so it's no surprise that fried fish is a popular dish on the island. Fresh fish is typically caught daily and fried to perfection. Fried fish is typically served with johnny cakes and a side of coleslaw or potato salad.

Price range: $15-$20 Location: Fried fish can be found at most restaurants in Anguilla, but some of the best places to try it include:

Palm Grove Bar and Grill (Sandy Ground)

Ocean Echo (West End)

SunShine Shack (Meads Bay)

BBQ Chicken

BBQ chicken is another popular dish in Anguilla. The chicken is typically marinated in a mixture of spices and then grilled over charcoal. BBQ chicken is typically served with johnny cakes and a side of coleslaw or potato salad.

Price range: $15-$20 Location: BBQ chicken can be found at most restaurants in Anguilla, but some of the best places to try it include:

Jelly BBQ (Sandy Ground)

Ken's BBQ (Sandy Ground)

Elvis Beach Bar (Sandy Ground)

Curried Goat

Curried goat is a flavorful and hearty dish that is popular in many Caribbean islands. The goat is typically marinated in a mixture of spices and then cooked in a curry sauce. Curried goat is typically served with rice and peas.

Price range: $15-$20 Location: Curried goat can be found at most restaurants in Anguilla, but some of the best places to try it include:

Tasty's Restaurant (Sandy Ground)

Roy's Bayside Grill (West End)

The Barrel Stay (Sandy Ground)

Stewed Oxtail

Stewed oxtail is a hearty and flavorful dish that is made with oxtail, vegetables, and a variety of spices. The oxtail is typically stewed for several hours until it is tender and juicy. Stewed oxtail is typically served with rice and peas.

Price range: $20-$25 Location: Stewed oxtail can be found at most restaurants in Anguilla, but some of the best places to try it include:

Tasty's Restaurant (Sandy Ground)

Roy's Bayside Grill (West End)

The Barrel Stay (Sandy Ground)

Grilled Lobster

Anguilla is known for its fresh lobster, and grilled lobster is a popular dish on the island. The lobster is typically grilled to perfection and served with a variety of sides, such as rice and peas, vegetables, or mashed potatoes.

Price range: $40-$50 Location: Grilled lobster can be found at most restaurants in Anguilla, but some of the best places to try it include:

Veya (West End)

Jacala (Shoal Bay East)

Scilly Cay (Scilly Cay)

These are just a few of the many delicious local Anguillan dishes that you can try. With its rich culinary culture, Anguilla has something to offer everyone.

6.2. Best Restaurants And Dining Options

Anguilla is a small island in the Caribbean with a reputation for world-class dining. The island has a wide variety of restaurants to choose from, offering everything from casual beachfront eateries to fine dining establishments.

Here are some of the best Anguilla restaurants and dining options, along with their location:

Fine Dining

Veya (West End): Veya is one of the most acclaimed restaurants in Anguilla, serving modern Caribbean cuisine in a romantic setting.

Jacala (Shoal Bay East): Jacala is another popular fine dining restaurant, offering a tasting menu of creative dishes made with fresh, local ingredients.

Scilly Cay (Scilly Cay): Scilly Cay is a unique dining experience, located on a small island just off the coast of Anguilla. The restaurant offers fresh seafood, grilled to perfection.

Casual Dining

Tasty's Restaurant (Sandy Ground): Tasty's is a popular spot for local Anguillan cuisine. The restaurant serves a variety of dishes, including pigeon peas and rice, curried goat, and stewed oxtail.

Roy's Bayside Grill (West End): Roy's Bayside Grill is a great place to enjoy a casual meal with a view. The restaurant offers a variety of dishes, including fresh seafood, sandwiches, and burgers.

The Barrel Stay (Sandy Ground): The Barrel Stay is a popular spot for both locals and tourists. The restaurant offers a variety of dishes, including pizzas, burgers, and seafood.

Other Dining Options

Beach Bars: Anguilla has a number of great beach bars where you can enjoy a casual meal and drinks with a view. Some popular beach bars include SunShine Shack, Elvis Beach Bar, and Sandy Island.

Food Trucks: Anguilla also has a number of food trucks that serve a variety of delicious dishes. Some popular food trucks include Tasty's Food Truck, Ken's BBQ, and Jelly BBQ.

No matter what your budget or taste, you're sure to find a great place to eat in Anguilla. Here are a few additional tips for planning your dining experience:

Make reservations: Many of the popular restaurants in Anguilla book up quickly, especially during peak season. It's a good idea to make reservations in advance, especially if you're dining at a fine dining restaurant.

Try the local cuisine: Anguilla has a rich culinary culture, so be sure to try some of the local dishes. Some popular local dishes include pigeon peas and rice, curried goat, and stewed oxtail.

Don't be afraid to ask for recommendations: The locals are always happy to recommend their favorite restaurants. If you're not sure where to eat, ask your hotel concierge or a local resident for their recommendations.

With its wide variety of restaurants and dining options, Anguilla is a great place to experience the Caribbean's culinary culture.

6.3. Food Festivals And Events

Anguilla is a small island in the Caribbean with a rich culinary culture. The island hosts a number of food festivals and events throughout the year, celebrating its delicious cuisine and fresh, local ingredients.

Here are some of the best Anguilla food festivals and events:

Anguilla Culinary Experience (ACE): The Anguilla Culinary Experience is a four-day festival that celebrates the island's culinary culture. The festival features a variety of events, including chef dinners, cooking demonstrations, and beach barbecues. ACE is a great way to experience the best of Anguilla's food and drink.

Date: May 23-26, 2024 Location: Various locations throughout Anguilla.

Festival Del Mar: Festival Del Mar is a two-day festival that celebrates the island's fishing culture. The festival features a variety of events, including fishing tournaments, boat races, and food stalls. Festival Del Mar is a great way to experience the local culture and try some of the island's fresh seafood.

Date: Easter Weekend Location: Island Harbor.

Anguilla Summer Festival: The Anguilla Summer Festival is a two-week festival that celebrates the island's culture and heritage. The festival features a variety of events, including boat races, parades, and concerts. The Anguilla Summer Festival is a great time to experience

66

the island's lively atmosphere and try some of the local food.

Date: August 1-15, 2024 Location: Various locations throughout Anguilla.

Anegada Lobster Festival: The Anegada Lobster Festival is a one-day festival that celebrates the island's delicious lobster. The festival features a variety of events, including a lobster cook-off, live music, and dancing. The Anegada Lobster Festival is a great way to try some of the freshest lobster in the Caribbean.

Date: November 24, 2023 Location: Anegada.

These are just a few of the many food festivals and events that are held in Anguilla throughout the year. With its rich culinary culture, Anguilla is a great place to experience the Caribbean's delicious food and drink.

Here are a few additional tips for planning your trip to one of Anguilla's food festivals and events:

Book your accommodations early: The food festivals and events in Anguilla are popular, so it's a good idea to book your accommodations early, especially if you're traveling during peak season.

Purchase tickets in advance: Some of the food festivals and events in Anguilla require tickets, so it's a good idea to purchase them in advance, especially if you're attending one of the more popular events.

Bring cash: Many of the food stalls and vendors at the food festivals and events in Anguilla only accept cash, so be sure to bring some with you.

Wear comfortable shoes: You'll be doing a lot of walking at the food festivals and events in Anguilla, so be sure to wear comfortable shoes.

With its delicious food, vibrant atmosphere, and friendly people, Anguilla is a great place to experience a Caribbean food festival or event.

CHAPTER SEVEN

Culture And Entertainment

7.1. Arts And Crafts

Anguilla is a small island in the Caribbean with a rich culture and history. The island's arts and crafts scene is vibrant and diverse, with local artisans creating a variety of unique and beautiful items.

One of the most popular types of Anguillian arts and crafts is straw weaving. Straw weaving is a traditional skill that has been passed down from generation to generation. Anguillian straw weavers use locally grown straw to create a variety of items, including hats, baskets, mats, and other decorative items.

Another popular type of Anguillian arts and crafts is pottery. Anguillian potters use local clay to create a variety of functional and decorative items, such as bowls, plates, cups, and vases. Some Anguillian potters also create unique sculptures and other works of art.

In addition to straw weaving and pottery, Anguillian artisans also create a variety of other types of arts and crafts, including:

Wood carving: Anguillian wood carvers use locally grown wood to create a variety of items, such as statues, bowls, and other decorative items.

Jewelry making: Anguillian jewelry makers use a variety of materials, such as shells, pearls, and precious metals, to create unique and beautiful pieces of jewelry.

Textile arts: Anguillian textile artists use a variety of techniques, such as sewing, quilting, and crocheting, to create a variety of items, such as clothing, bags, and other accessories.

Anguillian arts and crafts can be found in a variety of places on the island, including:

The Anguilla Arts and Crafts Centre: This center is located in The Valley, the capital of Anguilla. It features a variety of arts and crafts from local artisans, including straw woven items, pottery, wood carvings, jewelry, and textile arts.

Art galleries: There are a number of art galleries in Anguilla that feature the work of local artists. Some of the most popular art galleries include the ALAK ART GALLERY and the Ani Art Academies Anguilla.

Gift shops: Many gift shops in Anguilla sell a variety of Anguillian arts and crafts. Some of the best places to find Anguillian arts and crafts in gift shops include Cheddie's Carving Studio and the Anguilla Souvenir Shop.

When visiting Anguilla, be sure to take some time to explore the island's vibrant arts and crafts scene. You're sure to find something unique and beautiful to take home with you.

Here are some additional details about Anguilla arts and crafts:

Anguillian straw weavers: Anguillian straw weavers use a variety of techniques to create their unique and beautiful items. One of the most popular techniques is called "coiling." In coiling, the weaver starts with a bundle of straw and coils it around itself to create a base. The weaver then adds additional coils of straw to build up the sides of the item. Another popular technique is called "plaiting." In plaiting, the weaver braids three or more strands of straw together to create a flat or three-dimensional shape.

Anguillian potters: Anguillian potters use a variety of clays to create their items. One of the most popular types of clay is called "red ochre clay." Red ochre clay is a reddish-brown clay that is found in abundance in Anguilla. Anguillian potters also use other types of clay, such as white clay and yellow clay.

Anguillian wood carvers: Anguillan wood carvers use a variety of woods to create their items. Some of the most popular types of wood include cedar, mahogany, and teak. Anguillian wood carvers use a variety of tools to carve their items, including chisels, hammers, and saws.

Anguillian jewelry makers: Anguillan jewelry makers use a variety of materials to create their items. Some of the most popular materials include shells, pearls, and precious metals, such as gold and silver. Anguillian jewelry makers use a variety of techniques to create their items, including soldering, wire wrapping, and beading.

Anguillian textile artists: Anguillan textile artists use a variety of techniques to create their items. Some of the most popular techniques include sewing, quilting, and crocheting. Anguillian textile artists use a variety of materials to create their items, such as cotton, linen, and wool.

Anguillian arts and crafts are a reflection of the island's rich culture and history. When you purchase an Anguillian arts and crafts item, you are supporting local artisans and taking home a piece of Anguilla with you.

7.2. Music And Festivals

Anguilla is a small island in the Caribbean with a vibrant music and festival scene. The island's music is influenced by a variety of genres, including reggae, soca, calypso, and jazz. Anguillian musicians perform at a variety of venues, including hotels, restaurants, and bars.

One of the most popular music festivals in Anguilla is the Moonsplash Festival. The Moonsplash Festival is a three-day music festival that takes place annually in March. The festival features a variety of Caribbean artists, including reggae, soca, and calypso musicians. The Moonsplash Festival is held at The Dune Preserve, a beautiful beachfront venue located on Rendezvous Bay.

Another popular music festival in Anguilla is the Anguilla Summer Festival. The Anguilla Summer Festival is a two-week festival that takes place annually in July and August. The festival features a variety of events, including boat races, street parades, and live music performances. The Anguilla Summer Festival is held in various locations around the island, including Sandy Ground Village and The Valley.

In addition to the Moonsplash Festival and the Anguilla Summer Festival, there are a number of other music festivals and events that take place in Anguilla throughout the year. Some of these other events include:

The Anguilla Jazz Festival: This festival takes place annually in February and features a variety of jazz musicians from around the world.

The Anguilla Blues Festival: This festival takes place annually in March and features a variety of blues musicians from around the world.

The Anguilla Seafood Festival: This festival takes place annually in April and features a variety of food and music events.

The Anguilla Day Celebration: This festival takes place annually on May 30th and features a variety of events, including parades, live music performances, and cultural demonstrations.

When visiting Anguilla, be sure to check out the island's vibrant music and festival scene. You're sure to find something to enjoy, no matter what your musical taste.

7.3. Museums And Historical Sites

Anguilla is a small island in the Caribbean with a rich history and culture. There are a number of museums and historical sites on the island that offer visitors a chance to learn more about Anguilla's past and present.

Here are some of the most popular museums and historical sites in Anguilla, with entry fee and safety information:

Anguilla National Trust

The Anguilla National Trust is a non-profit organization that is dedicated to protecting and preserving Anguilla's natural and cultural heritage. The Anguilla National Trust operates a number of museums and historical sites on the island, including:

Heritage Collection Museum: This museum is located in The Valley, the capital of Anguilla. It features a variety of exhibits in Anguilla's history and culture, including artifacts from the island's indigenous people and European settlers. Entry fee is $5 USD for adults and $2.50 USD for children.

Wallblake House: This historic house is located in The Valley. It was built in the 18th century and is now a museum that features exhibits in Anguilla's history and culture. Entry fee is $10 USD for adults and $5 USD for children.

Big Spring National Park: This park is located in Sandy Hill Village. It features a natural spring that was used by Anguillians for centuries. The park also has a museum that features exhibits in Anguilla's history and culture. Entry fee is $5 USD for adults and $2.50 USD for children.

The Old Government House:

This historic building is located in The Valley. It was built in the 18th century and served as the seat of government for Anguilla until 1976. It is now a museum that features exhibits in Anguilla's history and culture. Entry fee is $10 USD for adults and $5 USD for children.

The Anguilla Archaeological Museum:

This museum is located in The Valley. It features exhibits in Anguilla's archaeological history, including artifacts from the island's indigenous people and European settlers. Entry fee is $5 USD for adults and $2.50 USD for children.

The Anguilla Maritime Museum:

This museum is located in Sandy Ground Village. It features exhibits in Anguilla's maritime history, including artifacts from the island's shipping and fishing industries. Entry fee is $5 USD for adults and $2.50 USD for children.

Safety in Anguilla:

Anguilla is a safe island to visit. However, it is always important to be aware of your surroundings and take precautions to protect yourself and your belongings.

Some safety tips for visitors to Anguilla:

Keep your valuables close to you and don't leave them unattended.

Be careful when swimming in the ocean and be aware of currents and riptides.

Use sunscreen and drink plenty of water to avoid sunburn and dehydration.

Be respectful of the island's culture and customs.

By following these safety tips, you can help ensure a safe and enjoyable visit to Anguilla.

CHAPTER EIGHT

Shopping

8.1. Souvenirs And Gifts

Anguilla is a small island in the Caribbean with a lot to offer visitors, including beautiful beaches, crystal-clear waters, and delicious food. But what about souvenirs and gifts? Here is a guide to what to buy and where to find it in Anguilla:

Clothing and accessories

Anguilla has a variety of shops selling clothing and accessories, including t-shirts, hats, and swimwear with the Anguilla logo or other island-themed designs. You can also find more unique items such as handmade jewelry, bags, and scarves. Some popular shops to check out include:

Irie Life: This shop sells a variety of casual clothing and accessories with Anguilla-inspired designs.

Limin' Boutique: This boutique sells handmade jewelry and other accessories made with local materials.

The Gift Box: This gift shop sells a variety of items, including clothing, jewelry, and souvenirs.

Food and drinks

Anguilla is known for its delicious food, so it's no surprise that there are a number of shops selling food and drinks to take home with you. Some popular items include:

Anguillian sea salt: This unique salt is harvested from the surrounding waters and is a popular souvenir for foodies.

Anguillian rum: Anguilla produces a number of different rums, which are available for purchase at liquor stores and some gift shops.

Anguillian honey: Anguillan honey is made from local wildflowers and is known for its sweet and delicate flavor.

Other souvenirs

In addition to clothing, accessories, food, and drinks, there are a number of other souvenirs you can purchase in Anguilla. Some popular items include:

Handmade crafts: Anguilla has a number of talented artisans who create handmade crafts such as pottery, wood carvings, and paintings. You can find these crafts at local markets and gift shops.

Beach souvenirs: Anguilla has some of the most beautiful beaches in the world, so it's no surprise that there are a number of beach souvenirs available for purchase. These souvenirs include items such as seashells, driftwood, and beach towels.

Local art: Anguilla has a vibrant arts scene, and there are a number of galleries where you can purchase local art.

Where to buy souvenirs in Anguilla

You can find souvenirs in Anguilla at a variety of places, including:

Gift shops: There are a number of gift shops located throughout Anguilla, selling a variety of souvenirs.

Markets: Anguilla has a number of markets where you can find local produce, crafts, and other souvenirs.

Resorts and hotels: Many resorts and hotels in Anguilla have gift shops where you can purchase souvenirs.

Duty-free shops: There are a number of duty-free shops located at the airport, where you can purchase souvenirs at a discounted price.

Tips for buying souvenirs in Anguilla

Shop around and compare prices: There are a number of different places to buy souvenirs in Anguilla, so it's important to shop around and compare prices before you buy anything.

Buy local: Whenever possible, try to buy souvenirs that are made locally. This will help to support the local economy and ensure that you are getting a unique and authentic souvenir.

Haggle: Haggling is common in Anguilla, especially at markets. Don't be afraid to haggle with vendors to get a better price.

Be aware of customs restrictions: Before you leave Anguilla, be sure to check the customs restrictions for your home country. There may be restrictions on the types and quantities of souvenirs that you can bring back.

By following these tips, you can find the perfect souvenirs to take home from your trip to Anguilla.

8.2. Local Markets And Boutiques

Merchants Market Group: This market is located in The Valley and is open from 8am to 5pm, Monday through Saturday.

Albert Lake Marketplace: This market is located in The Quarter and is open from 8am to 5pm, Monday through Saturday.

Ashleys SuperMarket: This market is located in The Valley and is open from 7am to 10pm, seven days a week.

Best Buy West: This electronics store is located in The Valley and is open from 9am to 7pm, Monday through Saturday.

Best Buy: This electronics store is located in The Valley and is open from 9am to 7pm, Monday through Saturday.

Janvel's Boutique: This boutique is located in Blowing Point and is open from 9am to 6pm, Monday through Saturday.

Irie Life Boutique: This boutique is located in The Valley and is open from 10am to 5pm, Monday through Saturday.

Bijoux: This boutique is located in Sandy Ground and is open from 10am to 6pm, Monday through Saturday.

Limin' Boutique: This boutique is located in Rte 1 and is open from 10am to 6pm, Monday through Saturday.

Glam Boutique: This boutique is located in Lower South Hill and is open from 10am to 6pm, Monday through Saturday.

8.3 Tips For Perfect Shopping

Shop around and compare prices: There are a number of different places to shop in Anguilla, from duty-free shops to local boutiques. It's important to shop around and compare prices before you buy anything, especially if you're looking for a good deal.

Buy local: Whenever possible, try to buy souvenirs and other items that are made locally. This will help to support the local economy and ensure that you're getting a unique and authentic product.

Be aware of customs restrictions: Before you leave Anguilla, be sure to check the customs restrictions for your home country. There may be restrictions on the types and quantities of items that you can bring back.

Plan your shopping ahead of time: Decide what you're looking for before you go shopping. This will help you to avoid impulse purchases and save you time.

Bring cash: Many businesses in Anguilla prefer cash, so it's a good idea to bring some with you when you go shopping.

Be prepared to walk: Anguilla is a small island, but there are still a number of different shopping areas. Be prepared to do some walking, especially if you're looking for a specific item.

Take your time and enjoy yourself: Shopping in Anguilla should be a fun experience. Take your time and enjoy browsing the different shops and markets.

CHAPTER NINE

Practical Information

9.1. Health And Safety

Anguilla is a British Overseas Territory located in the Leeward Islands of the Caribbean. It is known for its beautiful beaches, crystal-clear waters, and laid-back atmosphere. While Anguilla is a relatively safe place to visit, there are a few things visitors should be aware of in order to stay healthy and safe during their trip.

Crime

Crime rates in Anguilla are generally low, but petty theft can occur, especially in tourist areas. Visitors should take precautions to protect their belongings, such as locking doors and windows when they are not in their room, avoiding walking alone at night, and not leaving valuables unattended at the beach.

Medical Facilities

Medical facilities in Anguilla are limited, so it is important to have travel insurance in case of a medical emergency. The island has one public hospital, the Princess Alexandra Hospital, which is located in the Valley. There are also a number of private clinics and doctors' offices. However, if you require specialist care, you may need to be evacuated to another island or country.

Water

The tap water in Anguilla is generally safe to drink, but it is always a good idea to boil or filter it before drinking, especially if you have a sensitive stomach. Bottled water is also widely available.

Food

The food in Anguilla is generally safe to eat, but it is important to avoid eating raw or undercooked food, especially seafood. It is also a good idea to avoid eating at street stalls or restaurants that do not look clean and hygienic.

Sun Safety

The sun in Anguilla can be very strong, so it is important to protect yourself from sunburn. Be sure to wear sunscreen with an SPF of 30 or higher, reapply sunscreen every two hours, and wear a hat and sunglasses.

Other Safety Tips

Be aware of your surroundings and avoid walking alone at night, especially in unlit areas.

Do not carry large amounts of cash or valuables with you.

Be careful when swimming in the ocean, especially if there are strong currents or waves.

Drink plenty of water and avoid alcohol in excess.

Be respectful of the local culture and customs.

9.2. Emergency Contacts

In the event of an emergency in Anguilla, it is important to know who to contact.

Police, Fire, Ambulance: 911

Royal Anguilla Police Force: +(1 264) 497 2333

Princess Alexandra Hospital: +(1 264) 497 2551

Department of Disaster Management: +(1 264) 476 3622

Her Majesty's Prison: +(1 264) 497 2333

Anguilla Sea Rescue: +(1 264) 497 5897

Anguilla Electricity Company: +(1 264) 497 2000

Anguilla Water Corporation: +(1 264) 497 2111

Anguilla Tourist Board: +(1 264) 497 2759

Other Useful Contacts

United States Embassy in Barbados, the Eastern Caribbean, and the OECS: +(1 246) 431 0225

United Kingdom High Commission in Barbados: +(1 246) 436 6660

Canadian High Commission in Barbados: +(1 246) 436 6600

Australian High Commission in Barbados: +(1 246) 436 6600

Tips for Calling Emergency Services

When calling emergency services in Anguilla, please be prepared to provide the following information:

Your name and contact information

The nature of the emergency

Your location

Any other relevant information, such as the number of casualties or the type of injuries

It is also important to stay calm and follow the instructions of the dispatcher.

9.3. Local Customs And Etiquette

Anguilla is a British Overseas Territory with a rich and unique culture. It is important to be respectful of local customs and etiquette when visiting Anguilla, in order to ensure a pleasant experience for yourself and the locals.

Greeting

Anguillans are generally friendly and welcoming people. It is customary to greet people with a handshake or a nod and a smile. If you are meeting someone for the first time, it is polite to use their title and surname. For example, you would say "Good morning, Mr. Smith" or "Good afternoon, Dr. Jones."

Dress Code

Anguilla is a casual island, and there is no need to dress up for most occasions. However, it is important to dress respectfully, especially when visiting religious sites or government offices. It is also advisable to cover up when walking around town, as Anguillans are generally conservative people.

Tipping

Tipping is not customary in Anguilla, but it is appreciated for good service. A tip of 10-15% is customary at restaurants, bars, and hotels. You may also want to tip taxi drivers, tour guides, and other service providers.

Public Behavior

Anguillans are generally polite and respectful people. It is important to be mindful of your behavior in public, and to avoid being loud or disruptive. It is also considered rude to talk on your phone while eating in a restaurant or bar.

Other Customs and Etiquette Tips

It is considered rude to refuse food or drink when offered by a local.

It is customary to take off your shoes before entering someone's home.

Be respectful of the environment and avoid littering.

Be aware of your surroundings and avoid walking alone at night.

Be respectful of the local culture and customs.

9.4. 3 To 6 Days Packing Essentials

Anguilla is a beautiful Caribbean island known for its white-sand beaches, crystal-clear waters, and laid-back atmosphere. When packing for a trip to Anguilla, it is important to keep the climate and activities in mind. The weather in Anguilla is warm and sunny year-round, with average temperatures ranging from 75 to 85 degrees Fahrenheit. The island is also prone to hurricanes during the Atlantic hurricane season, which runs from June to November.

Packing List for 3 to 6 Days in Anguilla

Clothing

- 7-10 days of clothing, including swimsuits, shorts, t-shirts, sundresses, and light pants.

- A light jacket or sweater for cooler evenings.

- A cover-up for walking around town.

- A dress for a nice dinner out.

- Comfortable shoes for walking and exploring.

- Sandals or flip-flops for the beach.

Accessories

- A hat and sunglasses to protect yourself from the sun.

- Insect repellent.

- Sunscreen with an SPF of 30 or higher.

- A beach towel.

- A camera.

- A reusable water bottle.

- Other Essentials

- Passport and other travel documents.

Travel insurance.

- Credit cards and cash.

- Medication (if needed).

- Personal toiletries.

Optional Items

- A snorkeling mask and fins.

- A book or e-reader.

- A travel journal.

- A pair of binoculars for birdwatching.

- A small first-aid kit.

Tips for Packing

Roll your clothes instead of folding them to save space in your suitcase.

Bring a carry-on bag with essential items in case your luggage is lost or delayed.

Pack light so that you don't have to pay baggage fees.

Consider bringing a waterproof backpack or dry bag for beach trips and activities.

Anguilla Packing List for Specific Activities

Here are some additional items you may want to pack depending on your activities in Anguilla:

Beaches: Sunscreen, hat, sunglasses, beach towel, swimsuit, cover-up, sandals or flip-flops.

Snorkeling: Snorkel mask, fins, sunscreen, hat, sunglasses.

Hiking: Comfortable shoes, water bottle, insect repellent, sunscreen, hat, sunglasses.

Biking: Comfortable shoes, sunscreen, hat, sunglasses, water bottle.

Fishing: Fishing gear, sunscreen, hat, sunglasses, insect repellent.

Sailing: Sunscreen, hat, sunglasses, water bottle, comfortable shoes.

Golfing: Golf clubs, golf balls, sunscreen, hat, sunglasses, water bottle.

By following this packing list, you can ensure that you have everything you need for a comfortable and enjoyable trip to Anguilla.

9.5. Visitor Information Centres

Anguilla, a British Overseas Territory in the Eastern Caribbean, is a popular tourist destination known for its stunning beaches, crystal-clear waters, and laid-back atmosphere. Visitors to Anguilla can learn more about the island's history, culture, and attractions at one of the two Visitor Information Centers located on the island.

The Valley Visitor Information Center

The Valley Visitor Information Center is located in the heart of the capital city, The Valley. It is open Monday to Friday from 8:00 AM to 5:00 PM and offers a variety of services to visitors, including:

Information on Anguilla's attractions, beaches, restaurants, and accommodations.

- Free maps and brochures

- Assistance with booking tours and activities

- Currency exchange

- Wi-Fi access

The Valley Visitor Information Center also has a small gift shop where visitors can purchase souvenirs, such as Anguillian crafts, clothing, and food products.

The Blowing Point Visitor Information Center

The Blowing Point Visitor Information Center is located at the Blowing Point Ferry Terminal, which is the main point of entry for visitors arriving to Anguilla by ferry from St. Maarten. It is open Monday to Sunday from 8:00 AM to 5:00 PM and offers the same services as the Valley Visitor Information Center.

Visitor Information Center Staff

The staff at both Visitor Information Centers are knowledgeable and friendly, and they are always happy to help visitors plan their trip and make the most of their time in Anguilla. Visitors can ask the staff questions about anything from the best places to snorkel to the best restaurants to try.

How to Get to the Visitor Information Centers

Both Visitor Information Centers are easily accessible by car or taxi. There is also a public bus service that stops near both centers.

Tips for Visiting the Visitor Information Centers

It is best to visit the Visitor Information Centers early in the day, especially if you are planning on booking tours or activities.

Be prepared to answer questions about your travel plans, such as how long you will be staying in Anguilla and what types of activities you are interested in.

If you have any specific questions about Anguilla, be sure to write them down so that you don't forget to ask them at the Visitor Information Center.

The Visitor Information Centers in Anguilla are a valuable resource for visitors to the island. By taking the time to visit a Visitor Information Center, visitors can learn more about Anguilla and plan their trip accordingly.

CHAPTER TEN
Itineraries

10.1. 3-Days Anguilla Adventure

Anguilla, a British Overseas Territory in the Eastern Caribbean, is a renowned tourist destination known for its stunning beaches, crystal-clear waters, and delicious food. With its laid-back atmosphere and friendly locals, Anguilla is the perfect place to relax and escape the hustle and bustle of everyday life.

If you're planning a trip to Anguilla, here is a possible itinerary for a 3-day adventure:

Day 1:

Morning: Arrive at Princess Juliana International Airport (SXM) in St. Maarten and take a ferry or sea shuttle to Anguilla. The journey takes around 20 minutes.

Afternoon: Check into your hotel and leave your luggage. Then, head to Shoal Bay Beach, one of the most popular beaches on the island. Spend the afternoon swimming, sunbathing, and people-watching.

Evening: Have dinner at one of the many excellent restaurants along Shoal Bay Beach. For a special occasion, try Dune Preserve, which offers stunning ocean views and a creative menu.

Day 2:

Morning: Take a boat trip to the Prickly Pear Cays, a pair of uninhabited islands located just off the coast of Anguilla. The islands are known for their white-sand beaches, turquoise waters, and excellent snorkeling opportunities.

Afternoon: Spend the afternoon relaxing on the beach, swimming, and snorkeling. If you're feeling adventurous, you can also try kayaking or paddleboarding.

Evening: Return to Anguilla and have dinner at one of the many restaurants in Sandy Ground, a charming village on the south side of the island. For a casual meal, try The Hungry Monkey, which serves up delicious Caribbean and international cuisine.

Day 3:

Morning: Visit the Anguilla Heritage Museum to learn about the island's history and culture. The museum is located in Wallblake House, a historic plantation house dating back to the 17th century.

Afternoon: Take a drive to Rendezvous Bay, a beautiful beach located on the north side of the island. Spend the afternoon swimming, sunbathing, and reading a book.

Evening: Have dinner at one of the many restaurants in West End, a lively village located on the west side of the island. For a romantic meal, try Blanchard's, which offers fine dining and stunning ocean views.

This is just a suggested itinerary, of course. You can customize it to fit your interests and budget. For example, if you're interested in history, you could spend more time at the Anguilla Heritage Museum or visit some of the island's other historical sites, such as Fort George or Wallblake House. If you're on a tight budget, you could eat at less expensive restaurants or pack your own lunches and snacks.

No matter what you choose to do, you're sure to have a wonderful time in Anguilla. It's a truly special place with something to offer everyone.

10.2. Romantic Getaway

Anguilla is a British Overseas Territory in the Eastern Caribbean, and it's a renowned tourist destination known for its stunning beaches, crystal-clear waters, and delicious food. With its laid-back atmosphere and friendly locals, Anguilla is the perfect place to relax and escape the hustle and bustle of everyday life.

If you're planning a romantic getaway to Anguilla, here is a possible itinerary:

Day 1:

Morning: Arrive at Princess Juliana International Airport (SXM) in St. Maarten and take a ferry or sea shuttle to Anguilla. The journey takes around 20 minutes.

Afternoon: Check into your hotel and leave your luggage. Then, head to Meads Bay, one of the most beautiful beaches on the island. Spend the afternoon swimming, sunbathing, and strolling along the beach hand-in-hand.

Evening: Have dinner at one of the many excellent restaurants along Meads Bay Beach. For a romantic meal, try Straw Hat, which offers fine dining and stunning ocean views.

Day 2:

Morning: Take a couple's massage at one of Anguilla's many luxury spas. This is the perfect way to relax and pamper yourselves.

Afternoon: Take a boat trip to Sandy Island, a small uninhabited island located just off the coast of Anguilla. The island is known for its white-sand beaches, turquoise waters, and excellent snorkeling opportunities.

Evening: Have dinner at one of the many restaurants in Sandy Ground, a charming village on the south side of the island. For a casual meal, try Tasty's, which serves up delicious Caribbean and international cuisine.

Day 3:

Morning: Visit the Anguilla National Trust's Nature Discovery Centre to learn about the island's unique flora and fauna. The center also has a number of hiking trails that you can explore together.

Afternoon: Take a cooking class together and learn how to make some of Anguilla's delicious dishes. This is a fun and interactive way to learn more about the island's culture.

Evening: Have dinner at one of the many restaurants in West End, a lively village located on the west side of the island. For a romantic meal, try Veya, which offers fine dining and a creative menu.

This is just a suggested itinerary, of course. You can customize it to fit your interests and budget. For example, if you're interested in history, you could visit the Anguilla Heritage Museum or Fort George. If you're on a tight budget, you could eat at less expensive restaurants or pack your own lunches and snacks.

No matter what you choose to do, you're sure to have a wonderful time on your romantic getaway to Anguilla. It's a truly special place with something to offer everyone.

Here are some additional tips for planning a romantic getaway to Anguilla:

Book a room at a romantic hotel or resort. There are many excellent options to choose from, such as Cap Juluca, A Belmond Hotel, Anguilla; Malliouhana Resort; or Zemi Beach House, LXR Hotels & Resorts.

Plan some special activities for two, such as a couples massage, a boat trip to a secluded island, or a cooking class together.

Make reservations at some of Anguilla's best restaurants. The island has a thriving culinary scene, so there are many options to choose from, whether you're looking for a romantic meal or a casual bite to eat.

Pack your swimsuits, sunscreen, and insect repellent. Anguilla is a tropical island, so it's important to be prepared for the hot weather and sun.

Relax and enjoy each other's company. Anguilla is the perfect place to escape the hustle and bustle of everyday life and reconnect with your loved one.

10.3. Family-Friendly Excursions

Anguilla is a British Overseas Territory in the Eastern Caribbean, and it's a renowned tourist destination known for its stunning beaches, crystal-clear waters, and delicious food. It's also a great place to visit for families, with plenty of family-friendly activities and excursions to choose from.

Here are a few ideas for family-friendly excursions in Anguilla:

Visit the beach. Anguilla has some of the most beautiful beaches in the Caribbean, and they're perfect for swimming, sunbathing, and building sandcastles. Some of the most popular family-friendly beaches include Shoal Bay Beach, Meads Bay, and Rendezvous Bay.

Go snorkeling or diving. Anguilla's coral reefs are home to a variety of marine life, including colorful fish, sea turtles, and rays. There are a number of tour operators that offer snorkeling and diving excursions for families.

Take a boat trip to the Prickly Pear Cays. The Prickly Pear Cays are a pair of uninhabited islands located just off the coast of Anguilla. They're known for their white-sand beaches, turquoise waters, and excellent snorkeling opportunities.

Visit the Anguilla National Trust's Nature Discovery Centre. The Nature Discovery Centre is a great place to learn about Anguilla's unique flora and fauna. It also has a number of interactive exhibits and activities that are perfect for kids.

Take a cooking class together. Anguilla has a thriving culinary scene, and there are a number of cooking schools that offer classes for families. This is a fun and interactive way to learn about the island's culture and cuisine.

Copyrighted Page

In addition to these specific excursions, there are many other family-friendly activities to enjoy in Anguilla, such as:

- Visiting the Anguilla Heritage Museum

- Taking a nature walk through one of the island's many national parks

- Playing mini golf at Anchor Miniature Golf

- Visiting the Anguilla Animal Rescue Centre

- Going shopping in the villages of Sandy Ground and West End

No matter what your family's interests are, you're sure to find something to enjoy in Anguilla. It's a great place to create lasting memories with your loved ones.

Here are a few additional tips for planning a family-friendly vacation to Anguilla:

Choose a hotel or resort that is family-friendly. Many hotels and resorts in Anguilla offer amenities and activities that are specifically designed for families, such as kids' clubs, swimming pools, and playgrounds.

Copyrighted Page

Pack plenty of sunscreen, insect repellent, and hats for everyone in your family. Anguilla is a tropical island, so it's important to be protected from the sun and mosquitoes.

Bring snacks and drinks for your kids, especially if you're planning on spending long days at the beach or on excursions.

Take breaks throughout the day. Anguilla is a hot and humid island, so it's important to stay hydrated and take breaks from the sun.

Be flexible with your plans. Things don't always go according to plan on vacation, so it's important to be flexible and go with the flow.

With its stunning beaches, crystal-clear waters, and friendly locals, Anguilla is the perfect place for a family-friendly vacation.

CHAPTER ELEVEN

Conclusion And Travel Tips

12.1. Final Thoughts

As we conclude this journey through the captivating island of Anguilla, it's impossible not to reflect on the myriad experiences, breathtaking landscapes, and warm hospitality that this Caribbean gem offers. Anguilla, often referred to as the "Tranquil Isle," is not just a destination; it's a sanctuary for those seeking an escape from the ordinary. In this final section of our travel guide, we aim to encapsulate the essence of Anguilla and leave you with a lasting impression of this island paradise.

Anguilla's beauty is undoubtedly one of its most defining features. With its powdery white-sand beaches stretching out as far as the eye can see and crystal-clear turquoise waters, it's a place where the visual allure transcends mere words. From the iconic Meads Bay to the serene Shoal Bay East, and the secluded Maundays Bay, every beach has a unique charm that beckons visitors to unwind, soak up the sun, and take in the tranquility. The picture-perfect sunsets over the horizon are nothing short of magical, making Anguilla an ideal backdrop for romance and relaxation.

Beyond its stunning coastline, Anguilla's cultural diversity is a treasure waiting to be explored. The island's history is rich, reflecting the influences of the Arawaks, Caribs, African slaves, and European colonizers. This amalgamation of cultures is vividly expressed through the island's music, art, and cuisine. Don't miss the opportunity to savor the delectable flavors of Anguillian cuisine, which often feature fresh seafood, flavorful spices, and a fusion of Caribbean and international influences. Restaurants and beachside shacks alike offer a culinary journey that is nothing short of unforgettable.

A visit to Anguilla wouldn't be complete without delving into the lively local culture. The warmth of the Anguillian people is infectious, and their genuine smiles and welcoming demeanor make every traveler feel like a friend. You can engage with the community at local festivals, such as the lively August Monday parade or the soothing sounds of the Moonsplash Music Festival. These events offer a glimpse into the heart and soul of the island, where music, dance, and camaraderie flourish.

For the adventure seekers, Anguilla offers a range of activities that provide an adrenaline rush and an opportunity to explore the island from a different perspective. Snorkeling and diving enthusiasts can explore vibrant coral reefs and underwater caves teeming with marine life. Watersports such as paddleboarding and kite surfing are readily available, allowing you to ride the waves of the Caribbean Sea. Nature lovers can venture into Anguilla's untamed landscapes, exploring hidden trails and pristine national parks.

When it comes to accommodation, Anguilla provides a spectrum of options to cater to various preferences and budgets. From luxurious beachfront resorts offering unparalleled opulence to cozy boutique hotels and charming guesthouses, there's a place to call home for everyone.

In conclusion, Anguilla is a destination where dreams come true. It's a place where the simplicity of life, the embrace of nature, and the warmth of its people combine to create an unforgettable travel experience. Whether you seek relaxation on pristine beaches, adventure in the depths of the Caribbean Sea, or a cultural immersion into the heart of the island, Anguilla delivers. It's a world unto itself, a place where time slows down, and serenity reigns supreme.

We hope this travel guide has provided you with the knowledge and inspiration to embark on your own journey to Anguilla. The memories you create on this tranquil isle will undoubtedly linger in your heart, calling you back to its shores again and again. Anguilla is not just a destination; it's a promise of an extraordinary, unforgettable experience that will leave you yearning for more. So, pack your bags, leave your worries behind, and let the magic of Anguilla envelop you in its timeless embrace.

12.2. Travel Tips For An Unforgettable Experience

Anguilla is a British Overseas Territory in the Caribbean, known for its stunning white-sand beaches, crystal-clear waters, and laid-back atmosphere. Whether you're looking for a relaxing beach vacation, an adventurous getaway, or a cultural immersion, Anguilla has something to offer everyone.

Here are some tips for planning an unforgettable trip to Anguilla:

Getting there

The best way to get to Anguilla is by flying into Clayton J. Lloyd International Airport (AXA). There are direct flights from several major US cities, including Miami, New York, and Newark. You can also take a ferry from St. Maarten, which is just a short boat ride away.

When to go

Anguilla has a tropical climate with warm temperatures year-round. The best time to visit is during the dry season, from December to May. However, the island is also beautiful during the summer months, although it can be more humid and rainy.

Where to stay

Anguilla has a wide range of accommodation options, from budget-friendly guesthouses to luxurious resorts. Some popular areas to stay include Shoal Bay, Meads Bay, and Sandy Ground.

What to do

Anguilla is a great place to relax and enjoy the beach. But there are also plenty of other things to see and do, such as:

Snorkeling and diving in the crystal-clear waters

Sailing and kayaking around the island

Visiting the Anguilla National Trust's Wallblake House and Heritage Museum

Exploring the quaint villages of Sandy Hill and The Valley

Enjoying a sunset cocktail at one of the many beachfront bars and restaurants

Food and drink

Anguilla has a vibrant culinary scene, with a wide range of restaurants to choose from. Be sure to try some of the local dishes, such as Anguillan crayfish, johnnycakes, and rum punch.

Other tips

Anguilla is a relatively expensive island, so be prepared to spend a bit more than you would on other Caribbean islands.

The island is on Eastern Caribbean time, which is four hours ahead of Coordinated Universal Time (UTC).

The official currency of Anguilla is the East Caribbean dollar (XCD). However, US dollars are widely accepted.

Anguilla is a relatively safe island, but it's always a good idea to be aware of your surroundings and take precautions against petty theft.

Here are some additional tips for having an unforgettable experience in Anguilla:

Talk to the locals. Anguillians are known for their friendly and welcoming nature. Don't be afraid to strike up a conversation with a local to learn more about the island and its culture.

Get off the beaten path. Anguilla has many hidden gems, such as secluded beaches, charming villages, and local restaurants. Venture away from the tourist hotspots to experience the real Anguilla.

Embrace the island time. Anguilla is a laid-back island, so don't be in a hurry. Slow down, relax, and enjoy the moment.

With its stunning beaches, crystal-clear waters, and friendly people, Anguilla is the perfect destination for an unforgettable Caribbean vacation. Follow these tips to plan your dream trip and create memories that will last a lifetime.

NOTE

DATE...............

_____

_____

_____

_____

_____

_____

_____

_____

_____

_____

_____

_____

NOTE

DATE................

NOTE

DATE................

Made in the USA
Monee, IL
09 January 2024

51469577R00066